GEORGE ORWELL

The Complete Poetry

Compiled and presented

by

Dione Venables

with an introduction

by

Peter Davison

*

f

Poems by George Orwell
Copyright © The estate of the late Sonia Brownell Orwell
Text copyright © Dione Venables
Preface copyright © Peter Davison
Poem by Jacintha Buddicom copyright © Dione Venables

ISBN 978-0-9553708-2-3

First published in 2015 by Finlay Publisher for The Orwell Society

The right of Dione Venables to be identified as the author of this work has been asserted by her in accordance with the Copyright, Designs and Patents Act 1988.

All rights reserved. No part of this publication may be produced in any form or by any means – graphic, electronic or mechanical including photocopying, recording, taping or information storage and retrieval systems – without the prior permission, in writing, of the publisher.

A CIP catalogue record of this book
can be obtained from the British Library.

Book designed by Michael Walsh
at The Better Book Company
and printed by ImprintDigital.com

Dedicated with affection
to Richard Blair
who loves to read
his father's poetry.

WEST SUSSEX **LIBRARY SERVICE**	
201608043	
Askews & Holts	13-May-2016
821.91	

"…….I do not want completely to abandon the world-view that I acquired in childhood. So long as I remain alive and well I shall continue to feel strongly about prose style, to love the surface of the earth, and to take pleasure in solid objects and scraps of useless information. It is no use trying to suppress that side of myself."

From 'Why I Write'. Orwell wrote this essay for *Gangrel* in the summer of 1946.

CONTENTS

Foreword .... *i*
Preface .... *v*
Abbreviations 57
Textual Notes 58
Index of First Lines 61
Acknowledgements 63

*

'Awake! Young Men of England'(2 October 1914) 1
Kitchener (21 July 1916) 2
Song 1.Come Up, Come Up, Ye Kindly Waves
    (from 1916-1918) 4
Song 2 Three Beggars Begged by Noon & Night
    (1916-1918) 5
The Pagan (Autumn 1918) 7
Our Minds are Married (Christmas 1918) 9
To A.R.H.B. (27 June 1919) 9
Wall Game (29 November 1919) 10
After Twelve (1 April 1920) 12
Ode to Field Days (1 April 1920) 13
The Photographer (9 July 1920) 14
The Wounded Cricketer (9 July 1920) 15
The Youthful Mariner (Extract 1920) 16
Friendship and Love (Summer 1921) 18
Jacintha's Reply (Summer 1921) 19
Dear Friend: Allow Me For a Little While
    (Burma 1922?) 19
Romance. Burma (1922-1927?) 20
When the Franks Have Lost Their Sway
    (Burma 1922-1927?) 21
Brush Your Teeth (Burma 1922-1927?) 23
The Lesser Evil (Burma 1927?) 23

My Love and I Walked in The Dark (Burma 1927?)........25
John Flory: Epitaph 27
King Charles ll: song by Sir John Digby (Autumn 1930) 28
Sometimes in the Middle Autumn Days (March 1933)....28
Summer For an Instant (May 1933) 30
A Dressed Man and a Naked Man (October 1933) 31
from Burmese Days: J. Flory couplet....................................33
On a Ruined Farm Near His Master's Voice Gramophone
    Factory, (*The Adelphi.* April 1934)..............................34
St Andrew's Day, November 1935..36
Advertisement: Why Should You be Thin and White?
    (*Keep the Aspidistra Flying.* 1936)..................................37
A Happy Vicar I Might Have Been (November 1936).......38
Limericks...40
Scraps of Nonsense Poetry:.......................................40
The Italian Soldier (Autumn 1942)...41
As One Combatant to Another;
    Letter to 'Obadiah Hornbooke' (*Tribune* 1943)........43
Memories of the Blitz (*Tribune* Jan. 1944)...........................48
Beasts of England (*Animal Farm* 1945)................................50
Animal Farm couplet 1945 51
Comrade Napoleon (*Animal Farm* 1945)...............................51
Were There Always These Vistas
    (*Nineteen Eighty-Four* 1949)..53
Song:Under the Spreading Chestnut Tree (*1984*) 1949...54
Epitaph to Joseph Higgs. 1949...............................54

*

Foreword

When setting out to gather in all of George Orwell's poetry, both good and not so good, it should be recognized why anyone would bother to do this. He was not a major poet, and some might suggest that he was not even a minor one of any merit. But those critics would be wrong. Eric Blair, who later became George Orwell, scattered poetry throughout his work in every possible form, as liberally as a chef adds sugar and spices to his dishes, even dedicating one of his essays to this art form ('Poetry and the Microphone.' GO Essays. *Penguin Classics.* 2000. p 239). Yet very little of his poetry is recognized and, although the occasional emotional line is quoted, few can identify the poem from which it is referenced.

It was because of the steady trickle of worldwide enquiries from members and non-members of the Orwell Society that this little book is being published. Each query has asked for a certain reference to be identified as being by Orwell (or not) and that the name of the particular poem and its location be supplied. Such requests have meant that many hours have had to be spent in hunting through the 20 volumes of *George Orwell: The Complete Works*, compiled and edited by Professor Peter Davison (assisted by Ian Angus and Sheila Davison), only to discover that the line in question is nowhere to be found. At other times it will be successfully located and then the poem can be identified and passed on to whoever has asked for clarity. This kind of enquiry is welcome, but is so expensive in terms of time that it gradually began to dawn that there should be a reference book of *all* of Orwell's poetry, not just the more popular ones, to enable readers to look up his complete poetical works and find the quotation for themselves.

Some of the blame for the neglect of Orwell's poetry, of course, falls upon the man himself, because it has to be acknowledged that there is some indifferent material between these covers. However, it is safe to promise that the reader, though possibly occasionally exasperated, will suddenly come upon a verse or even a line whose beauty, poignance or perfect choice of words simply take the breath away. Poetry tends to do that to the reader, because it is generated purely by emotion which ensures the depth of the great divide between it and the regular written word. The fact remains that George Orwell composed these poems and they should be accessible. *George Orwell: The Complete Poetry* will, I believe, provide a useful source for academics, libraries, students and readers of poetry generally.

In *The Collected Essays, Journalism & Letters*, edited by Sonia Orwell & Ian Angus (Vol IV, pp 418-419), Orwell says in a letter to George Woodcock in April 1948, when sent some of his verses to read:

> '... I think you should make your mind up a bit better on the subject of rhyme. Part of the time you use ordinary rhymes, but a good deal of the time assonances like thought-white, hours-fears, etc; I must say, I am against this kind of rhyme, which seems to me only, as it were, an intellectual rhyme, existing on paper because we can see that the final consonant is the same. The lack of rhymes in English is a very serious difficulty, and gets more serious all the time, as familiar rhymes get more and more hackneyed, but I have always felt that if one is to use imperfect rhymes it would be better to make the vowel sound and not the consonant the same, e.g. open-broken, fate-shape, sound to me more like rhymes than eye-voice, town-again, and so forth. However, I'm no judge of such things.'

He did judge 'such things' all the same, and his own verses are remarkably free of this kind of liberal indulgence. Orwell felt that poetry was in decline in the Western world when he wrote about it (see above). He quoted Arnold Bennett's opinion, saying that 'Bennett had hardly exaggerated when he said that 'in the English-speaking countries the word "poetry" would disperse a crowd quicker than a fire-hose.' Fortunately, since then, such programmes as *Poetry Please* on BBC Radio 4 has done much to re-kindle our interest and affection for poetry.

I have, for many years, done my best to read George Orwell's poetry wherever I could find it, now and then discussing it with others. Their response was usually either completely negative or else a vague remembrance of a much quoted line, like the last lines in the poem about the Italian soldier in the Spanish Civil War[1].

> 'No bomb that ever burst
> Shattered the crystal spirit.'

George Woodcock made that last line the title of his book when writing about his friend George Orwell (*The Crystal Spirit*, Jonathan Cape 1969). I am grateful to his memory for focusing my attention on Orwell's emotive use of the English language within his poetry and, from it, being able to share such occasional diamonds with those who will take the time to read through this collection.

How many readers can identify where the following verse comes from?

> 'Sometimes in the middle autumn days,
> The windless days when the swallows have flown,
> And the sere elms brood in the mist,
> Each tree a being, rapt, alone.'

Then, again a simple couplet:

> 'Christ! How they huddled up to one another
> Like day-old chicks about their foster-mother.'

Or even a single line, and it is safe to assume that very few readers will have come across this before;

'Seven separate pains played in his body like an orchestra.'

That line has gripped me since I first read it; has stamped itself on my memory. It reveals the situation within Orwell himself at the end of his life when he was struggling for the energy to merely breathe, and still having to deal with the other warning pains in his failing body. These are the poems that are known to so few that everyone has the right to know about, and upon which to make their own judgement.

As George Orwell, then Eric Blair, had such an emotionally poetic first love with his muse Jacintha Buddicom, I had very much hoped that it would be possible to unearth a similar exchange between Eric and Eileen O'Shaughnessey whom he married in 1936. She was always interested in poetry, and even wrote a poem in her schooldays entitled '1984,' so I am sure that such poems were exchanged during their courtship, but they have not so far come to light. There is always hope.

Special emphasis has been given to the introductions and footnotes accompanying every poem, because they are essential in bringing the circumstances surrounding each subject into focus. Here and there, it has been possible to link a poem with a response. In providing this kind of background detail, it is hoped that a little more light will be cast upon the mood in which each poem was written, underlying the depth of emotions littering Orwell's brief but bountiful life.

I would like to reiterate that all opinions offered within these pages are entirely my own, unless otherwise identified.

Dione Venables
Chichester
January 2015

PREFACE

Orwell and poetry

It is for his prose that Orwell is particularly – and rightly – admired. He wrote rapidly – perhaps when under pressure to fulfil the demands of journalism sometimes too rapidly – but his love of poetry and his urge to write poetry began at a very early age and, as his final notebooks show, never left him. Indeed, I think it might be claimed that that love of poetry – of words and their sounds – influenced his prose.

In his essay, 'Why I Write' Orwell describes his first attempts at creative writing. These were centred on poetry. In that essay he famously stated 'I knew I had a facility with words and a power of facing unpleasant facts' – itself a fascinating conjunction which characterises his writing throughout his life. He goes on, 'I wrote my first poem' – and note, when he begins to write it is poetry that he attempts – 'at the age of four or five, my mother taking it down to dictation. I cannot remember anything about it except that it was about a tiger and the tiger had "chair-like teeth" – a good enough phrase, but I fancy the poem was a plagiarism of Blake's "Tiger, Tiger". When he was eleven he wrote the first poem in this collection. When he was a little older he wrote what he calls 'bad and usually unfinished "nature poems" in the Georgian style'. He later produced *vers d'occasion*, 'semi-comic poems which I could turn out at what now seems to me astonishing speed'. By the time he was sixteen 'I suddenly discovered the joy of mere words, i.e. the sounds and associations of words'. (CW, XVIII, 316-7).

Although his metier would be in prose, in revitalising the essay and the art of the causerie, a love of poetry never left him. To the very end of his life he was attempting to write poetry. His Last Literary Notebook has a sketch for a poem marked by black humour – 'Joseph Higgs, late of this parish'. A 'learned' element that could lurk beneath the surface in Orwell pops up here with its quotation from Thomas of Celano's thirteenth-century Mass of the Dead: 'Ne me perdas illa die' (Do not destroy me on that day). Surely an ironic quotation in the light of Orwell's own condition at this time!

Among the books that Orwell read in 1949 were William Empson's *Seven Types of Ambiguity* and he 'skimmed' through Cleanth Brooks's *Modern Poetry and the Tradition* – surely serious reading for a very sick man? He also read T.S. Eliot's 'From Poe to Valéry' in which Eliot writes, 'In the *Biographia Literaria* Coleridge is concerned primarily, of course, with the poetry of Wordsworth; and he did not pursue his philosophical enquiries concurrently with the writing of his poetry; but he does anticipate the question that fascinated Valéry: "What am I doing when I write a poem?" Is it too much to suggest that Orwell posed that question to himself not only in his attempts at poetry but with regard to all his writing?

In the autumn of 1940 Orwell was approached by the BBC to discuss the proletarian writer in a broadcast with C. V. Hawkins. That evidently went well enough for him to be approached in the early spring of 1941 by Z. A Bokhari to give four broadcasts on literary criticism. The third of these was on 'The Meaning of a Poem' and was broadcast on 14 May 1941. The poem he chose was Gerard Manley Hopkins's 'Felix Randal'. He explains that this is generally regarded as a 'difficult' poem and at the end of the broadcast he explains why this is so – because of its emphasis on the use of words of Saxon rather than Norman French origin. There is, he says, a class distinction between the two. 'Many agricultural labourers speak almost pure Saxon' – and Hopkins's language is very Saxon tending to string several English words together 'instead of using a single long Latin one, as most people do when they want to express a complicated thought'. Thus the poem is a synthesis of a special vocabulary and a special religious and social outlook. 'The two fuse together, inseparably, and the whole is greater than the parts'. What is significant in this context of Orwell as poet is not so much his analysis of 'Felix Randal' but the degree to which it indicates Orwell's fascination with language and its use in a poetic medium. Orwell's writing is not like this – he is rightly famed for the simplicity, clarity and directness of expression – but it does reveal how he saw and might interpret the poetic medium.

Paradoxically, Orwell's most sustained interest in poetry in so far as it is represented in his work was during the time that he was ostensibly involved in what was intended as propaganda: his work for the BBC Overseas Service to India and the East. Laurence Brander, the BBC's Eastern Service Intelligence Officer, a friend of Orwell's and author of one of the first biographies of Orwell in 1954, only touches briefly on the broadcast of poetry in his 'Report on Indian Programmes', 11 January 1943, but he points out that the Delhi office is 'run by a distinguished Urdu writer' (Ahmed Ali), and that through him 'we can get recordings made – if we can afford the money to do so.' He concludes, 'If we can arrange to acquire recordings of the best poets it will give us a long lead over any radio competitors' (XV, 349-50).

Orwell had a carbon copy amongst his papers at his death of a slightly earlier report on the preferences of the English-speaking audience as to whether listeners preferred to hear Indian or English voices; 55% preferred English voices and only 13% Indian voices. Furthermore 80% preferred news bulletins read by those with English voices. (It was less flattering to Orwell in answers to the question which personalities were most enjoyed. He achieved only 16% whereas J.B. Priestley scored 68%, Dr C.E.M. Joad 56%, and E.M. Forster 52%.) An even earlier report, and Brander's first, which Orwell almost certainly read (because it is concerned with broadcasters in his charge) was written from New Delhi on 12 May 1942.

It is not known whether Orwell read the report which refers to the broadcasting of poetry but it is inconceivable that he and Brander did not discuss the issues his reports raise. Who influenced whom is impossible to tell but what we do know is that on 11 August 1942 Orwell launched what, for the BBC, was a completely innovative series of six broadcasts: a literary magazine programme called 'Voice' which made a speciality of broadcasting readings and discussing contemporary poetry. Poems included those written by Herbert Read, Dylan Thomas, Edmund Blunden, W.H. Auden, Stephen Spender and T.S. Eliot (his 'Love Song of J. Alfred Prufrock' and 'The Journey of the Magi').

Among the many programmes – the prototype of 'distance learning' – that Orwell created for Indian students was a series of seven devoted to modern English verse, the first programme being an introduction by Orwell broadcast on 13 June 1943. Among the poetry featured was that of T.S. Eliot, W.H. Auden, the Georgians, War Poets, and the Apocalyptics. The fascinating initial proposal for this series of broadcasts has survived (13 April 1943) with full details of proposed topics and speakers and the many, many poets to be included (XV, 62-64).

How did Orwell look back on this innovatory experience? In a fascinating essay, 'Poetry and the Microphone', possibly written in the summer of 1943, he discussed what he had learned. This was published, as so often with Orwell, in a 'little magazine', *New Saxon Pamphlets*, in March 1945 (CW, XVII, pp. 74-80; reprinted in my collection, *Orwell's England*, Penguin, 2001). I would hazard a guess that what most people remember from it, if they know the essay at all, is his description of that 'grisly thing, a "poetry reading"' often conducted in an atmosphere of 'frigid embarrassment'. Orwell makes a strong case for reading poetry over the radio – he was writing when television was unavailable.

The essay is too long to summarise in detail here but one or two salient points are worth mentioning. First he notes that 'the audience is conjectural, but it is an audience of one', or at most, a small group. Each listener will feel addressed individually. Further, the speaker – if possible the author – will soon realise that *'the audience has no power over you'*; the broadcaster does not have to take his tone from the audience – in effect to accommodate 'the stupidest person present'. There will be no need for the speaker to ingratiate himself or herself 'by means of the ballyhoo known as "personality".' He goes on to discuss the way the whole subject of poetry can be seen as 'embarrassing, almost indecent, 'as though popularising poetry were essentially a strategic manoeuvre', and he quotes Arnold Bennett as 'hardly exaggerating when he said that in the English-speaking countries the word "poetry" would disperse a crowd quicker than a fire hose'.

There is considerably more to this essay but I hope I have referred to enough to indicate how important poetry was to Orwell and how much he wished that his love of poetry were more widely shared. But, in passing, especially given that poetry is more openly discussed and heard now, it is an example of how his time broadcasting to India should not be regarded – as it was by Orwell himself – as 'two wasted years'.

I cannot conclude without indulging myself in selecting a few poems which give me particular pleasure. My reasons for selecting these are not strictly their poetic qualities but the associations they have for me and which may explain why they still mean so much to me.

'Awake! Young Men of England'

It is not so much as a poem, nor because it was Orwell's first published work, that these lines are memorable to me. I am fortunate to live in Marlborough and the College is one of those schools, like Orwell's Eton, that boys so rapidly, oh! so rapidly and fatally, rushed to the colours in 1914. Like so many other boys from schools public and state, who went off to fight with such high hopes, huge numbers did not come back – no fewer than 749 from Marlborough – and many came back shattered. At the school I attended with such little distinction we had masters who had fought in that war. Two I recall vividly: one had served with Allenby in Palestine and another had been badly gassed. But these tyro verses also recall to me school friends who were killed in the Second World War, including one shot down over Sicily, two of the three head boys in my time, both inspirational young men, and my housemaster, C.V. Carlin, who went down with HMS *Hood*.

On a Ruined Farm Near His Master's Voice Gramophone Factory

Like the first poem, this, peaceful though it is, takes me back to war, this time World War Two. Shortly before I joined the Royal Navy, I was working in the cutting rooms of the Crown Film Unit at Pinewood Studios. If German planes were seen to be coming in our direction at Pinewood, an alarm was sounded and those who wished to do so could take to the shelters. The V-1 – the Flying Bomb or Doodlebug – allowed no such time to take cover. If an attack was expected, to save time being wasted, someone was posted high up on one of the film stages to keep look-out and warn if V-1s were coming in our direction. I was positioned on the top of a stage on 7 July 1944 when I saw in the distance one such Flying Bomb. I don't recall whether or not I sounded the alarm but I did see it fall some five miles short of where I was perched. It landed on the HMV Gramophone Factory at Hayes, Middlesex. It missed the main building but succeeded in killing over forty people and upwards of thirty more were injured enough to require hospital treatment.

The poem, despite being written ten years earlier, has curious echoes of that attack – 'My mortal sickness how I give – stuffless ghosts – the acid smoke – the winged soul –

their spirit free – Faith, and accepted destiny' It may seem to be stretching the imagination too far, but I still feel that event of 1944 seventy years on.

Memories of the Blitz

This poem, published in *Tribune* on 21 January 1944, stands isolated from the rest of Orwell's poetry. It encapsulates perfectly the weariness the war aroused as we entered its fifth year. It has also, so typical of Orwell's character, a delightful touch of humour – the study of the male and female snore! – coupled with a sense of that utter waste brought on by 'casual slaughter' and the general feeling of a world run-down – even the barrage balloon has a patched fabric at its nose. I was fortunate not to be living in the worst bombed areas though we had a barrage balloon parked outside our house and a mobile anti-aircraft gun that dashed up and down our road. And my school was fire-bombed and an aerial mine missed the building in which I was sleeping by a yard or two. Obviously I was lucky and yet this poem brings back vividly so much of the feeling of waste and despair that one had to fight against almost as much as the more obvious physical enemies. And that 'bigamous sparrow': what a splendid *envoi*!

A Happy Vicar I Might Have Been

Orwell here juxtaposes our easy acceptance of life when times seem good, but concealing from ourselves the threat of the commissar, and our maiming of our joys, or our hiding them. It encapsulates so much of the mid-thirties yet still speaks forcefully to me today.

'The Italian Soldier'

These nine verses have no title but conclude Orwell's essay, 'Looking Back on the Spanish War'. They are, I think, worthy of inclusion in any anthology but I have an additional and personal reason for selecting them. Early in World War

2 several of our teachers were called up. The art master, Mr Eastman, was taken prisoner at Dunkirk and spent the war in a prison camp forging papers for escapees. Inevitably, although some of the substitutes were brilliant – the very best was our one and only lady teacher – some were not. It was soon apparent that our replacement French teacher, Mr Cule, was incapable of controlling us. To my shame, I joined in with others in ragging him. This was particularly sad because he was good at the teaching itself and, even sadder, because he was obviously suffering physically as a result of his experiences fighting in the Spanish Civil War. If he told us about that war, we listened – enthralled; if poor Molecule as we called him, tried to teach us French, there was a riot. Alas, he had to go. But I have felt my share of blame ever since and Orwell's wonderful poem brings home to me my shameful part in his treatment. It was an insight into mob behaviour that has remained with me.

There is an expressive contrast throughout the poem between hope and loss – the soldier is dead and he and Orwell are fighting for what they hope will be a world more just and less treacherous. But 'luck is not for the brave' and 'the lie that slew you is buried / Under a deeper lie'. And the final stanza is, I find, unutterably moving. Here is Orwell the poet! But the poem also stands for me as a permanent rebuke.

—o—

I do not doubt that my enjoyment and appreciation of Orwell as poet is to a large extent dictated by the personal associations some of his poems have for me – associations which, I confess, are irrelevant to the poetry in its own right. But it may well be that his love of poetry and his lifelong attempts to write it are chiefly significant for the way it honed his skills as a master of prose. In addition, it can be claimed that his broadcasting of poetry and how he saw that that might be developed has had a long-standing influence from which we still benefit.

Peter Davison
6 February 2015

O*n the 2 October, 1914*, a poem was published in *The Henley & South Oxfordshire Standard*, just under eight weeks after the declaration of war between the nations of the British Empire and Germany. It was submitted by Master Eric Blair, the eleven-year-old son of Mr R.W. Blair of Rose Lawn, Shiplake.

'Awake! Young Men of England'

*

Oh! give me the strength of the lion,
The wisdom of Reynard the fox,
And then I'll hurl troops at the Germans,
And give them the hardest of knocks.

Oh! think of the War Lord's mailed fist,
That is striking at England today,
And think of the lives that our soldiers
Are fearlessly throwing away.

Awake! oh you young men of England,
For if, when your Country's in need
You do not enlist by the thousand,
You truly are cowards indeed.

Eric Blair.

At the time this poem was accepted by his local newspaper, Eric Blair had, since the age of eight, been a pupil at St. Cyprian's preparatory boarding school in Eastbourne on the East Sussex coast of the United Kingdom, so this first success at being published came from a 'seasoned' scholar in his third year away from home. It had previously been assumed that St. Cyprian's would have provided much of the influence fueling this fiery 'call to arms', but an article written by Peter Duby and published in *The Orwell Society Newsletter* (Issue 4 July 2014) suggests that the *crise de guerre* came from within his own family.

Eric's first cousin, Neville Lascelles Ward, killed during the Battle of Mons, on the 23 August 1914, was one of the first British soldiers to lose his life in the First World War. He had graduated from Sandhurst and, as a 2nd lieutenant with the East Surrey Regiment, had been sent to France as part of the first wave of the British Expeditionary Force. He and many of his platoon were cut off and engulfed by the German advance through Belgium into Northern France. Neville Ward was twenty years of age when he died, only nine years older than Eric, so it might well have been the first time that Eric had experienced the grief of the death of a member of his family. It was enough, together with the shock of his mother's and his aunts' mourning, to ignite an intense patriotism in him; an emotion which seems to have prevailed as he matured.

Two years later, following the death at sea of Earl Kitchener (1850-1916), Eric was stirred once more to mourn the death of Great Britain's national treasure, when his class were given the set work of celebrating the life of 'The Hero of Khartoum'. Four years at St. Cyprian's had done much to expand both his horizons and his vocabulary, and when the poem appeared in *The Henley and South Oxfordshire Standard* on the 21st July 1916, 'Master Eric Blair' had become the more adult-sounding E.A. Blair.

'Kitchener'

*

No stone is set to mark his nation's loss,
No stately tomb enshrines his noble breast,
Not e'en the tribute of a wooden cross
Can mark this hero's rest.

He needs them not; his name ungarnished stands
Remindful of the mighty deeds he worked,
Footprints of one, upon time's changeful sands,
Who n'er his duty shirked.

> Who follows in his steps no danger shuns,
> Nor stoops to conquer by a shameful deed.
> An honest and unselfish race he runs,
> From fear and malice freed.

Although he 'borrowed' a popular phrase in verse three (line 2) straight from the title of Oliver Goldsmith's 18th century comedy, thereby illustrating the breadth of education the school was giving its pupils, no one seems to have picked this up. Eric was to borrow from similar styles in some of his later school publications.

Several life-long friendships were forged at St. Cyprian's, despite Eric's apparent hatred of the place, and maybe the closest of them was with the literary critic and writer Cyril Connolly. Eric followed Connolly to Eton and their association continued until Eric's death in January 1950. Since both boys created Kitchener poems, it is interesting to note that, in a letter to his mother, Connolly commented that 'Blair did a very good poem which he sent to his local paper where they took it.'[2]

In September 1914 the way that Eric spent his school holidays changed. He decided to introduce himself to a family of three children who lived on the other side of the hedge at the end of the garden of Rose Lawn, Shiplake, which the Blair family had rented earlier in the year. He had watched their energetic games, probably noting that they were close to his own age, although he was taller than the elder girl, and her brother. The smaller girl would have been little older than Avril, his younger sister who was six years old and inclined to follow him around. The rapport and laughter he heard and watched must have drawn him like a moth to the flame, so he approached them and found them friendly and welcoming. This was the beginning of his friendship with the Buddicom family.

The three Buddicoms were all 'bookish.' Their mother was a published writer, their father a geologist, their grandparents all highly educated and scholarly, so 'learning' had begun in the cradle. The siblings, however, all had a flair for gaiety and fun, and clearly enjoyed each other's company. Eric could not resist them and very soon became the fourth member of the group, with the occasional addition of the much more reserved Avril.

When the weather was good they roamed the fields and fished in the river Thames at Upper Shiplake. When grey wet days kept them indoors, Eric was introduced to complicated 'parlour games', and a constant flow of poetry writing, stories to tell each other, and plays to perform together during the winter holidays. There is no indication that Eric wrote his early plays to share with the Buddicoms, but the timing suggests that this was a possibility. Jacintha, the elder Buddicom daughter and two years older than Eric, was very interested in play performance, historical magic, in the mysteries of Merlin, and the ghost and horror stories flooding the market in that era. Whatever the reason, around the time that Eric completed his primary education at St. Cyprian's in 1916 and was waiting to hear whether he would be going to Wellington College or Eton, he produced a colourful, even flamboyant, play for Christmas which features two 'songs'. Just how impressionable Eric was at this age is reflected in Jacintha's own collected volume of poetry from 1915-1986. From about thirteen years of age Jacintha wrote and sang her songs and Eric would have been as enchanted by them as he was with her. From his play 'The Man and the Maid', the hero Lucius sings this to his sorcerer father Miraldo:

'Song (1)'
*

Come up, Come up, ye kindly waves,
and wash the cold sea sand.
Come kiss the shore that I live on
For ye are come from land.

> Oh happy waves that ride so free
> and know not rain nor fear!
> While I must stay & watch ye break,
> For the strong Fates hold me here.
>
> Oh send me help from out your deeps,
> And I will weep no more.
> For fish-tailed maid or wingèd horse
> Would bear me safe to shore.
>
> Oh look on me again, hard Fates,
> And stay my father's hand:
> And the gay sea that tumbles here
> Shall bear me yet to land.

These dramatic words suggest bold gestures and flashing eyes, and despair mingled with longing. Eric, having caught his mother's habit of using the ampersand in mid-sentence, was testing his vocabulary, giving full rein to drama and imagination – no holds barred. It feels as though he was suddenly revelling in the sheer excess of glorious words, of exaggeration and florid passion. He was, after all, approaching thirteen at this time. The second 'song' also shows that he was beginning to pay attention to the beauty of rhythm in his words and was even confident enough to give a wryly humorous twist to the last line:

'Song (2)'

*

> Three beggars begged by noon & night,
> They begged to left & they begged to right,
> But nought had got for their trouble:
> So two sat them down & wept full sore,
> But the third one said they should weep no more
> And vowed they should yet feed double.

> They parted ways at the rise of sun,
> And swore to meet when the day was done,
>   And each should tell his findings.
> So one went east & one went west,
> But the third went on, for he thought it best,
>   And followed the path way's windings.
>
> They met on the road as the sun went down,
> Back from the field & back from the town,
>   And two came slow & sadly.
> But the third was filled with wine & meat
> His face was calm & his voice was sweet,
>   And he tripped his way right gladly.
>
> 'Oh what hast thou?' said the last to the first,
> 'Alack' said he, 'my fate was the worst,
>   'T'was naught but blows & kicking.
> A few little scraps of cold pork fat,
> And a handful of bones I stole from a cat
>   Were all I had for my picking.'
>
> "Alas,' said the second, 'the same had I;
> Nor bread, nor meat, nor pudding, nor pie,
>   No food what e'er I did – o.'
> 'But I,' said the third, 'sat me down to dine,
> And I have had meat, & I have had wine,
>   For I went to the house of the widow.'

What a delight to discover in so young a poet, however Edwardian and florid his verse, the first gleam of that wry and mischievous humour for which Eric's friends and readers would love him in later years. It was something that the Buddicoms most enjoyed about their new friend and which they would recall with affection thirty years after his death.

By 1918 Eric was seriously in love. Letters between Jacintha and her later reminiscences, and that of her younger sister Guiny (Guinever) suggest that this was almost inevitable. Eric was always tall for his age and Jacintha was always small and very petite. She was extremely intelligent, had a lovely singing voice, and a great compassion and affection for animals. She was, even as a teenager, a questioning Christian, filled with doubts and arguments with which Eric agreed. Although he enjoyed her brother Prosper's company, when the two boys would go off with their shotguns to shoot birds or any small thing that moved, during their summer visits to Ticklerton (the Buddicom grandfather's home in Shropshire), it was with Jacintha that he liked best to walk and talk and create poetry. There was a lake (Soudley Pool) at Ticklerton where they went to fish and sometimes to picnic in the long grass where the trees bowed over the lake. Close to the water was a glade which, in spring, was carpeted with bluebells and they would lie amongst them, immersed in the intoxication of the bruised flowers' bitter-sweet scent. [3] This was possibly where Eric began to regard Jacintha as his Muse. After one such holiday he returned to Eton and wrote her a poem with not a single ampersand in sight, recalling an evening at the end of the school holidays when they went mushrooming in the fields north of Shiplake by Harpesden Woods, and sat in a stubble field to watch a particularly glorious sunset.

'The Pagan'

*

So here are you, and here am I,
Where we may thank our gods to be,
Above the earth, beneath the sky,
Naked souls alive and free.
The Autumn wind goes rustling by
And stirs the stubble at our feet;
Out of the west it whispering blows,
Stops to caress and onward goes,
Bringing its earthy odours sweet.

> See with what pride the setting sun
> Kinglike in gold and purple dies,
> And like a rope of rainbow spun
> Tinges the earth with shades divine.
> That mystic light is in your eyes
> And ever in your heart will shine.

This declaration made a considerable impression on Jacintha, despite the fact that her muted response was to suggest a few changes, including removing the word 'naked' which she thought might give a wrong impression. However, it really was the first love poem she had ever received and was also the first love poem that Eric had ever written. As she later commented in her memoir *Eric & Us*, 'At the time we watched that sunset, we both said we would never forget it, and I never have.' She was a little more expansive (but not much more) when she mentioned this moment to me, many years later. She said an unforgettable thing in a thoughtful, dreamy way. 'You never forget those amber moments.'[4] What a beautiful expression this is, encasing forever a treasured event in the amber translucence of the memory.

Every school holiday the three young Buddicoms and Eric Blair were constant companions and, in the summer, made regular visits to Grandfather Buddicom's family home at Ticklerton, where A.E. Housmann came alive for Eric.

In the meantime, Eric's feelings for Jacintha were intensifying. He does not seem to have discussed her with Cyril Connolly or any of his other school friends; he kept her, and his feelings for her, very much to himself. It does appear though, from this next offering, that he could, even at such an early age, see Jacintha becoming a permanent part of his life.

'Our Minds are Married, but We are too Young.'
(Christmas 1918)

*

Our Minds are married, but we are too young
For wedlock by the customs of this age.
When parent homes pen each in separate cage
And only supper-earning songs are sung.

Times past, when medieval woods were green,
Babes were betrothed and that betrothal brief.
Remember Romeo in love and grief –
Those star-crossed lovers – Juliet was fourteen.

Times past, the caveman by his new-found fire
Rested beside his mate in woodsmoke's scent.
By our own fireside we shall rest, content
Fifty years hence keep troth with heart's desire.

We shall remember, when our hair is white,
These clouded days revealed in radiant light.

There are various poems possibly or probably attributed to Eric Blair in Volume 10 of *The Complete Works of George Orwell*.[5] It has been decided to reproduce those deemed to have *probably* been written by him. His emerging style is, after careful study, usually possible to recognize in his poems written for *College Days*, the Eton Magazine.

'To A.R.H.B'

*

Who is the mighty Captain? Who is he
That every Upper Boat doth wish to be?
'Tis he who sets the Ark a stroke sublime
To which they vainly try to keep in time.
'Tis he who puts up notices galore,
Then changes his great mind and puts up more;

> Who fines us heavily for damaging
> Our boats, or oars, or sculls, or anything;
> Who scorns the rules so slavishly obeyed
> By lesser lights than he; who's not afraid
> To put a dry-bob in the Boats, if so
> It pleases him, and even makes him row;
> Who's great enough to scorn such petty rules,
> Only laid down for novices and fools.
> This is the mighty Captain, this is he
> That every Upper Boat doth wish to be.

*

In the twentieth century all schools learned the same poetry, songs, hymns and biographies and this piece seems to have been inspired by the ballad 'Who is Sylvia?' by William Shakespeare. The greater part of the College Days poetry appears to be deliberately parodying all that the boys were being taught and, no doubt, the masters made little of this. At least it showed that their work had been absorbed, whichever way it was being interpreted. Take a look at the next example.

'Wall Game' [6]
(29 November 1919)

*

> If you can keep your face, when all about you
> Are doing their level best to push it in.
> If you can swear (though, swearing, all men doubt you)
> It wasn't you who slicked the keeper's shin,
> If you can furk and not get killed while furking,
> Or being fisted, fist 'em back again,
> Or can invent convenient aunts, thus shirking
> An afternoon of mud, and blood, and rain.
> If you can play without too great disaster,
> Or even try to think you like the game,
> If you can meet with Mixed Wall and with Master,
> And treat those two imposters just the same,

> If you can bear to have the shy you're claiming,
> Not given, the Lord – and referee – know why,
> Or miss the blasted goal at which you're aiming,
> Because the ball went half-an-inch too high,
> If you can gently moderate your lingo
> So as to turn the common bargee pink,
> And, when rebuked, reply, "I said, 'By Jingo'
> Four times, no more and 'Brother' twice, I think."
> If you can force your wall and fly and second
> To do your job long after they are done,
> And still hold on, when hours since they had reckoned
> The time for holding would be past and gone.
> If you can play at third and keep your shirt new,
> Or flying-man, nor lose the common clutch,
> If neither fists nor fearsome feet can hurt you,
> But you can hurt all men, though not too much,
> If you can fill the unforgiving minute
> With sixty second's worth of slaughter done,
> Yours is the game and everything that's in it,
> And you may wear your College Wall, my son.

*

This piece has the style and rhythm of that great poem *If* by Rudyard Kipling (1865-1936) and illustrates that Eric still considered Kipling to be one of his most respected poets at that stage. He then went on to have a love-hate regard for Kipling for the rest of his life. See an essay he wrote for *Horizon* in February 1942 which can be found in the 1986 Penguin Classics publication of George Orwell: Essays.

There is a poem in *College Days* which has a distinct ring of Blair but which has not been verified. It is in *The Complete Works* (Vol X. p 62-3) as being *possibly* by Eric Blair. It is included here on that understanding.

'After Twelve'
(*College Days* No: 4, 1 April 1920)

"Oh, what can ail thee, loafer lorn,
　　Alone, thy visage overcast?
The crowd has ebbed from Cannon Yard,
　　And third School's past.

"Oh, what can ail thee, loafer lorn,
　　So haggard and so woebegone?
The Bar in Tap is nearly full,
　　And the Bill's near done."

"I saw a cake in Fuller's shop,
　　Full, beautiful, of pinkish hue
And set with green angelica,
　　And violets too.

"I bought it from the shopman straight,
　　To take it home, a joy to eat,
I looked on it with eyes of love,
　　And smiled full sweet.

"I set it in a paper bag,
　　And nothing else in rapture saw.
When lo! there stood a master stern
　　Without the door.

"And there he took my name and House,
　　And there I dreamed – ah woe betide! –
The saddest dream I ever dreamed
　　On the High Street's side.

"I saw young boys, and older too,
　　Pale prisoners, death-pale were they all,
Who cried, 'The rules of Sunday bounds

>   Have thee in thrall.'
>
> "And that is why I sojourn here,
> Alone and pale by school-yard gates,
> The last boy's coming off the Bill,
>   And the fusee waits."

This strange 'episode' apparently relates to one of the masters at Eton, who had 'a tendency to be over-fond of some of the boys.' (Quoted from an explanatory footnote in *The Complete Works*, Vol X. p.62). Eric was at the time the co-editor of *College Days* and, with his co-editor away at the time, had to face the wrath of the Master in College alone for publishing such satirical material.

> 'Ode to Field Days'
> (College Days
> 1 April 1920)
> *

> Hills we have climbed and bogs we have sat in,
> Pools where we drenched our feet in mid-December,
> Trains we have packed, woods we have lost our hat in,
> When you are past and gone, we will remember.

> Oh open fields and dinner halting places,
> In the hot summer how we shall regret you!
> Oh nice bleak heaths and open windy spaces,
> Though you are lost to us, could we forget you?

> Stumbling on stones and falling over boulders,
> What pangs of grief the memory will bring us!
> Marching to trains with greatcoats on our shoulders,
> With what despair the loss of these will wring us.

> Oh summer haste to press thy footsteps past us,
> Speed the hot months we have to suffer yearly,

Bring back at last to thankful boys and masters
Those blessed field days that we love so dearly.

*

When reading through these early works it is interesting to hazard a guess at whose poetic style is being parodied, but *Ode to Field Days* surely emerged from Lawrence Binyon's famously patriotic poem '*For the Fallen*' which is still used every November on Remembrance Sunday in the United Kingdom. Binyon (1869-1943) published his poem in *The Times* on the 23 September 1914, six weeks after the start of the First World War.

'The Photographer'
(*College Days* No.5
9 July 1920)

*

Not a breath is heard, not a moving of lip,
As his hand stays poised o'er the shutter,
And only the gnat on the neck gives a nip,
And we think of the words we mayn't utter.

He develops them darkly at dead of night
In a little black hole of an attic;
He pulls all the curtains to shut out the light,
And stays there for ages, ecstatic.

He takes bits of paper and puts them in frames
And leaves them to print all the morning,
And thinks they'll be printed (and signed with our names),
The chemist or jeweller scorning.

But many and loud are the words he speaks,
And much more in anger than sorrow,

And he looks at the things he has worked at for weeks,
But he starts them again on the morrow.

We thought as we saw him undoing a clip,
As he walked unobserving towards us,
It was wiser no longer to stay, but to skip
For what refuge the gods might afford us.

Quickly and gaily we made our way,
and showed no traces of sadness,
For we felt we were free from his grasp for the day,
And we left him alone to his madness.

The timbre of this poem follows the rhythm of the epic poem by Charles Wolfe (1791-1823), *The Burial of Sir John Moore after Corunna*, familiar to school children and the many others who would have learned it in the first half of the 20th century. It must have especially appealed to Eric as he quoted it elsewhere to Steven Runciman.

'The Wounded Cricketer (Not by Walt Whitman)'
(*College Days* No.5
9 July 1920)

*

I am a wet-bob[7] who was trying to play cricket
(Not because I wanted to, but because I had to).
Then I got hit in the eye by a ball;
So I lie on the grass here under a lime tree,
The grass looks nice, and so does the sky too.
The leaves look green, and there are such lots of them.
One, two, three, four ... seven, eight, nine, ten,
... Eighteen, nineteen ... I can't count them.
The sky looks all blue and white and grey.

> I can hear someone walking on the road over there,
> His feet go up and down, up and down;
> He treads in the puddles and kicks the little pebbles, so that
> They rattle all over the place.
> The ground underneath me is all rough and humpy.
> I can feel a little beetle running down my backbone,
> And there's an ant on my ear.
> I can see a rook up there; he's black all over,
> I don't think I shall move: I feel nice and comfortable.

Eric was obviously enjoying the freedom from the restrictions of formal verse, although it feels as though he could not take it seriously. No doubt his enjoyment in writing this piece was probably greater than that of his readers. However, his pleasure in exploring other styles should not to be ignored. As he was probably learning Samuel Taylor Coleridge in 1920, the timbre and pace of 'The Rime of The Ancient Mariner' (1798) is easy to recognise in the following verses. See *George Orwell: The Complete Works* Vol X. No:55. Page 75.

'The Youthful Mariner (Extract)'
(*College Days*. No. 5
9 July 1920)

*

The Mariner blesseth the wind that helpeth him upon his way.	The sun shone out, the clouds went down, The wind sprang up behind; I blessed the wind that blew me on. And was so soft and kind.
	The boat clove through the rippling stream, And merrily splashed the oar; I blest the wind*, so soft and kind, And the boat that ran before
He inadvertently runneth upon a sand bank.	Then struck mine ear a jarring scrape Like wood that grinds on sand,

	And looking round, I lay aground And close beside the land.
And, when he hath righted himself, findeth that the good weather is changing.	I pushed her out with left-hand scull, And backed her down with right; But when I reached the middle stream The sun was out of sight.
The weather rapidly changeth for the worse.	The wind sprang up and blurred the stream And ever colder grew; The rising swell was rough as hell: Ye gods, but how it blew!
Until he is in danger of shipwreck.	The clouds were black, they whirled along, And madly ran the wave. Alas, thought I, that such a sky Should see me in my grave.
He turneth for home.	I turned for home, but still the flood Rose high and ever higher; It splashed my back and, cold as ice, It burnt my skin like fire.
But maketh	The rain came down by pints and quarts, And soaked me to the bone; The waves rose free and wild as the sea, And I was all alone.
Small progress.	My boat began to rock and sway, The water trickled in. Alas for home, in the leaping foam That drowned me with its din!
	Then on and on and down the stream That never seemed to end. (Suppose the boat had overturned! – But heav'n such thoughts forfend.)
He heareth the voice of a fellow sufferer.	Then in by bank, and down and down; The trees scarce let me pass. Then struck mine ear a human voice, Cried, "Look ahead, you ass!"

> Oh joyful sound that met mine ear!
> As sweet as wedding bell,
> That saved my mind in wave and wind,
> And very mouth of hell.

And, the weather abating, reacheth home safely.

> Then fell the wind and shone the sun
> At the kindly voice of man;
> And I was home from flood and foam
> Before Fourth School began.

*See Schoeffenheimer's Etymological Directory:
"I cannot find it in my mind to call it wind
But I can find it in my mind to call it wind."

*

The last poem Eric wrote to Jacintha Buddicom was in the summer of 1921 and must have been sent before the two families rented Glencroft, a house at Rickmansworth, Hertfordshire, for most of the summer holidays. He had completed his education at Eton and was facing up to his father's decision that he should enter the Civil Service and serve time in Burma, rather than continuing on to University. Jacintha had, the previous year, left Oxford High School for Girls and embarked upon her perilous journey through the Social Season of college balls, hunt balls, and what was known unofficially as 'The Marriage Market.' Had this poem been written any later, in view of what occurred during their stay in Rickmansworth, Jacintha would not have responded to it in the gently calming way with which her sparse, clever words deflected his ardour.

'Friendship and Love'
(summer 1921)

*

Friendship and love are closely intertwined,
My heart belongs to your befriending mind:
But chilling sunlit fields, cloud-shadows fall –
My love can't reach your heedless heart at all.

And Jacintha's reply:

> By light
> Too bright
> Are dazzled eyes betrayed:
> It's best
> To rest
> Content in tranquil shade.

Was this the reason for Eric's subsequent outburst during the last of their walks in the leafy Rickmansworth lanes; the consequence of which changed the direction of both their lives. [8]

The habit of thinking in poetic form, as the two young friends had done since childhood, was still very strong and for some time Eric must have been deeply mourning the loss of his Muse who had also been his closest confidante. One poem entitled 'Dear Friend, Allow Me for a Little While' is recorded in *George Orwell: The Complete Works*, Vol X (p. 89) which, with its raw pain, a couple of defiant ampersands and dripping with self-pity, might well have been created for Jacintha on Eric's return to England. When shown it many years later, she did not appear to recognize it, but it is not beyond the bounds of possibility that Jacintha, by then in her 70s, did receive the poem but found it too painful to 'remember'.

> 'Dear Friend: Allow Me for a Little While'
> (hand-written but not dated.)
>
> *
>
> Dear Friend: allow me for a little while
> To speak without those high and starry lies
> Wherein we use to drown our thoughts until
> Even ourselves believe them. Hear then, first,
> Not all the screams of twenty thousand victims
> Broken on the wheel or plunged in boiling oil

> Could pain me like one tooth in my own head;
> And secondly, I do not care what comes
> When I am gone, though kings or peoples rot,
> Though life itself grows old; I do not care
> Though all the streams & all the seas ran blood;
> I care not if ten myriad blazing stars
> Rain on the earth & burn it dead as stone;
> I care not if God dies. // And all because
> Frankly, & look at it the way you will,
> This life, this earth, this time will see me out,
> And that is all I care about.

Between 1922 and 1927, when Eric was serving in Burma, he wrote various poems which suggest his mood during that period. Although actual dates are not available, one has to consider that he had just spent weeks travelling by sea to the other side of the world, having been furiously rejected by his first real love. He was nineteen and rejection is at its most painful at such an age. Carrying this with him to Burma, it would not have taken long for him to be introduced by his colleagues to the local 'facilities'. Since the girls in Burma tended to be small and shapely, as Jacintha had been, his enjoyment of their company resounds throughout his verse – though he soon discovered the extent of their 'devotion', judging by the comic irony of the last two lines in the following poem.

'Romance'
(Burma 1922-1927?)
*

> When I was young and had no sense,
> In far off Mandalay
> I lost my heart to a Burmese girl
> As lovely as the day.

> Her skin was gold, her hair was jet,
> Her teeth were ivory;
> I said "For twenty silver pieces,
> Maiden, sleep with me."
>
> She looked at me, so pure, so sad,
> The loveliest thing alive,
> And in her lisping virgin voice,
> Stood out for twenty five.

Five years serving in Burma gave Eric plenty of time to think about the world around him. He had learned Burmese with ease and gained the confidence and friendship of certain Burmese officials, discovering how the British Raj 'dealt' with its Colonial peoples. It affected his early enjoyment of his position with the Indian Imperial Police, and may have accounted for the first nuance of bitterness in his poetry. It certainly gave him plenty of fuel to burn on the fires of his growing writing commitment. He soon learned to curb this style but it took him many years to hone his work into the crisp and uncluttered phrases for which he became revered.

> 'When the Franks Have Lost Their Sway.'
> (1922-1927)
> *
>
> When the Franks have lost their sway
> And their soldiers are slain or fled,
> When the ravisher has his way
> And the slayer's sword is red;
> When the last lone Englishman dies
> In the painted Hindu towers,
> Beneath ten thousand burning eyes
> In a rain of bloody flowers, or again
> Moving more westward to the land we know,
> When the people have won their dreams,

> And the tyrant's flag is down,
> When the blood is running in streams
> Through the gutters of London town;
> When the air is burst with the thunder
> And crash of the falling thrones,
> And the crack of the empires torn asunder
> And the dying tyrant's groans, when, as I said
> These things will happen, which, one fears, they may.
> Or, moving onward through the mist of time
> To watch the last wild ending of the world,
> When the birds fall out of the sky,
> And leaf is black on the tree,
> When the creatures of earth all die,
> And the ice grows over the sea;
> When the suns & moons in their flight
> Stand still at an icy breath,
> And the wheel of the day & the night
> Is locked in the freedom of death;
> When the toil of a thousand years
> Is lost in a second of time,
> When the hopes are gone with the fears
> And the prayer is vain as the rhyme;
> When the gods have had their day
> And Death with the others dies,
> When the stars are empty for ever & aye
> As they hang in the jet black skies, – oh my dear brethren
> Is it not dreadful thus to contemplate
> These mighty ills that will beset the world
> When we are dead & won't be bothered with them?
> Do not these future woes transcend our own?

A playful element in Eric Blair's poetry emerges now and then, especially at the beginning of his service with the Indian Imperial Police when the newness of his surroundings would have absorbed and fascinated him. He wrote before recording the following [9], "Long ago I used to chant this sometimes as I washed my teeth, but that is a practice I have abandoned for two years or more. My self-respect and my last tooth brush both wore out soon after I got here."

'Suggested by a Toothpaste Advertisement'
*

Brush your teeth up and down, brother,
Oh brush them up and down!
All the folks in London Town
Brush their teeth right up and down,
Oh! how they shine!
Aren't they bloody fine?
Night and morning, my brother,
Oh brush them up and down!

By the time he was due for home leave at the end of his five-year posting, Eric had once more begun to think of verdant England and the contrast between the exotic perfumed Asian country with which he had become so familiar, and the green and distant land of his birth.

'The Lesser Evil'
(1927?)
*

Empty as death and slow as pain
The days went by on leaden feet;
And parson's week had come again
As I walked down the little street.

Without, the weary doves were calling,
The sun burned on the banks of mud;
Within, old maids were caterwauling
A dismal tale of thorns and blood.

I thought of all the church bells ringing
In towns that Christian folk were in;

I heard the godly maidens singing;
I turned into the house of sin.

The house of sin was dark & mean,
With dying flowers round the door;
They spat their betel juice between
The rotten bamboos on the floor.

Why did I come, the woman cried,
So seldom to her beds of ease?
When I was not, her spirit died,
And would I give her ten rupees.

The weeks went by, and many a day
That black-haired woman did implore
Me as I hurried on my way
To come more often than before.

The days went by like dead leaves falling.
And parson's week came round again.
Once more devout old maids were bawling
Their ugly rhymes of death and pain.

The woman waited for me there
as down the little street I trod;
And musing on her oily hair,
I turned into the house of God.

*

On page 93 of *The Complete Works*, Vol X 'A Kind of Compulsion,' it states that stanzas four and five are handwritten replacements for what was originally typed:

The woman oiled her hair of coal,
She had no other occupation.

24

> She swore she loved me as her soul,
> She had no other conversation.

> The only thing that woman knew
> Was getting money out of men.
> Each time she swore she loved me true
> She struck me for another ten.

But then, following this, he reminisces on the poignant memories of those carefree years of early youth. It has been suggested that this next poem might have been written while Eric was still in Burma, when he was probably still hoping to be reunited with Jacintha on his return. One should not lose sight of the fact that he tried to get in touch with her as soon as his feet touched British soil. He telephoned the Buddicoms at Ticklerton and invited himself to their Shropshire home, hinting that he had brought a ring back for Jacintha. When he arrived he found that she was not there, and both Prosper and Guiny seemed unaccountably embarrassed at the very mention of her name. He returned immediately, in a very dark frame of mind, to London and the Buddicoms were never spoken of again in the Blair family until Eric's and Jacintha's late re-connection in 1949. (See *The Complete Works*, Vol XX)

'My Love & I Walked in the Dark'
(1922 – 1927?)

*

> My love & I walked in the dark
> Of many a scented night in June;
> My love & I did oft remark
> How yellow was the waning moon,
> How yellow was the moon.

> My love & I walked in the sun
> Of many a golden summer day;
> My love & I were quite as one
> To say how sweetly smelt the hay,
> How sweetly smelt the hay.
>
> And all throughout that pleasant while,
> When life & earth appeared so fair,
> My love & I did often smile
> To think what happy folks we were,
> What happy folks we were.
>
> But now, with one thing & another,
> When we are old & wise, it seems
> My love & I do never bother
> To talk upon those ancient themes.
> Those idle, ancient themes.
>
> The suns & moons are much the same,
> But all their golden charms are fled,
> And she & I look back in shame
> To think of all the things we said,
> The foolish things we said.

But Jacintha never 'looked back in shame.' She looked back at their childhood and teenage years rather with great regret, and years later, taking another admirer to Soudley Pool at Ticklerton, it was those magical years of her first love for Eric that remained in her memory.

While he was in Burma, Eric Blair began to write seriously, and a contemporary there, George Stuart, recalled that the original manuscript of *Burmese Days* was written in Katha (Qatar). (See interview in The Orwell Archive). It appears that Blair might have had a particular affiliation with this sad character in the Flory epitaph, who possibly represented all that Eric believed about himself during his five maturing years in India and Burma.

'JOHN FLORY'
Born 1890
Died of Drink 1927

*

"Here lie the bones of poor John Flory;
His story was the old old story.
Money, women, cards & gin
Were the four things that did him in.

He has spent sweat enough to swim in
Making love to stupid women;
He has known misery past thinking
In the dismal art of drinking.

Oh stranger as you voyage here
And read this welcome, shed no tear;
But take the single gift I give
And learn from me how not to live.

After his tramping experiences in Paris and London, and various places in between, from 1927 – 1930, Eric finally began to settle in to his adult life and decided to start by becoming a schoolmaster. [10] During this time he wrote a play for the boys in his care to perform as a Christmas play. It was called *Charles II* and, despite his own contempt for it, the play was apparently well received by its audience. It was performed again in April 1992 by the Compass Arts Theatre.

'Curtain Speech by Sir James Digby'

*

Good people all, this is a joyous time
When our good king, long in most dangerous plight,
Is safe at sea and bound for friendly France.
We'll honour it with song, and silver too
Sir Edward here and I will give you all
To drink good health unto his majesty.
Long may he flourish, and soon come the day
When the usurper Cromwell ends his sway, [11]
Peace, freedom and prosperity will reign
When England has her own true king again!
Come, sir, if you have a song, let's hear it.

Poetry had given way to prose by 1933 and Eric was turning out a steady stream of articles, reviews and essays for journals such as *Tribune*. However, now and then the varying intensity of life made him seek solace in poetry. In March 1933 *The Adelphi* published a poem that Eric, not yet George Orwell, had written. He was still teaching at The Hawthorns in Hayes, Middlesex and was constantly depressed by its stifling atmosphere. Adolf Hitler had made himself dictator and Chancellor of Germany. Eric's health was a constant problem, and Brenda Salkeld was still refusing to be persuaded into bed. His restless frustration glares from these lines:

'Sometimes in the Middle Autumn Days'
(*The Adelphi.* March 1933)

*

Sometimes in the middle autumn days,
The windless days when the swallows have flown,
And the sere elms brood in the mist,
Each tree a being, rapt, alone,

I know, not as in barren thought,
But wordlessly, as the bones know,
What quenching of my brain, what numbness,
Wait in the dark grave where I go.

And I see the people thronging the street,
The death-marked people, they and I
Goalless, rootless, like leaves drifting,
Blind to the earth and to the sky;

Nothing believing, nothing loving,
Not in joy, nor in pain, not heeding the stream
Of precious life that flows within us,
But fighting, toiling as in a dream.

Oh you who pass, halt and remember
What tyrant holds your life in bond;
Remember the fixed, reprieveless hour,
The crushing stroke, the dark beyond.

And let us know, as men condemned,
In peace and thrift of time stand still
To learn our world while yet we may,
And shape our souls, however ill;

And we will live, hand, eye and brain,
Piously, outwardly, ever-aware,
Till all our hours burn clear and brave
Like candle flames in windless air;

So shall we in the rout of life
Some thought, some faith, some meaning save,
And speak it once before we go
In silence to the silent grave.

*

However, Eric's mood visibly brightened soon afterwards when two months later, in May 1933, *The Adelphi* published another of his poems, this time written in an altogether lighter, more pastoral frame of mind. He was enjoying the company of various attractive female friends, such as Eleanor Jacques and Mabel Fierz, and still pursuing Brenda Salkeld with stoic determination.

'Summer For an Instant'

*

Summer-like for an instant the autumn sun bursts out,
And the light through the turning elms is green and clear;
It slants down the path and the ragged marigolds glow
Fiery again, last flames of the dying year.

A blue-tit darts with a flash of wings, to feed
Where the coconut hangs on the pear tree over the wall;
He digs at the meat like a tiny pickaxe tapping
With his needle-sharp beak as he clings to the swinging shell.

Then he runs up the trunk, sure-footed and sleek like a mouse,
And perches to sun himself; all his body and brain
Exalt in the sudden sunlight, gladly believing
That the cold is over and summer is here again.

But I see the umber clouds that drive for the sun
And a sorrow no argument ever can take away
Goes through my heart as I think of the nearing winter,
And the transient light that gleams like the ghost of May;

And the bird, unaware, blessing the summer eternal,
Joyfully labouring, proud of his strength, gay-plumed,
Unaware of the hawk and the snow and the frost-bound nights,
And of his death foredoomed.

*

The effort to write cheerfully was, however, just too difficult to sustain. Continually rebuffed by Brenda, and possibly depressed by his chronic lack of health, Eric reverted to the comfort of a doom-laden outlook. Those were the days before the nanny state ensured that no one need starve to death, and maybe this was written as he decided that he could no longer bear to teach at The Hawthornes, the private school in Hayes which still stuck to the outlook and disciplines of a former age. It was not yet possible to live off his literary earnings, despite the publication in England of *Down and Out in Paris and London* – with his new identity as George Orwell. By the time autumn became winter in 1933 his health had deteriorated and he went into hospital, suffering from pneumonia. The return to his parents' home for recovery was fortuitous because 1934 was the year when *A Clergyman's Daughter* was written, and during which *Burmese Days* was at last published, first by Harper & Brothers, New York and then by Gollancz in London. He was fit again by October and the launch of *Down and Out in Paris and London* in June 1933 in New York ensured that he was at last solvent enough to move to London. He took a room in Hampstead and found himself a job there as part-time assistant at Booklovers' Corner.[12] That year, when Eric became George, he felt optimistic enough to be able to send *The Adelphi* a much more up-beat offering.

'A Dressed Man and a Naked Man'
(*The Adelphi*, October 1933)

*

A dressed man and a naked man
Stood by the kip-house fire,
Watching the sooty cooking-pots
That bubble on the wire;

And bidding tanners up and down,
   Bargaining for a deal,
  Naked skin for empty skin,
   Clothes against a meal.

"Ten bob it is," the dressed man said,
  "These boots cost near a pound,
  "This coat's a blanket of itself
"When you kip on the frosty ground."

"One dollar," said the naked man,
  "And that's a hog too dear;
  "I've seen a man strip off his shirt
   "For a fag and a pot of beer."

"Eight and a tanner," the dressed man said,
  "And my life-work is yours,
  "All I've earned at the end of a life
   "Knocking at farmers' doors;

"Turnips, apples, hops and peas
"And the spike when times are slack,
  "Fifty years I've tobied it
"For these clothes upon my back."

"Take seven," said the naked man,
  "It's cold and the spikes are shut;
   "Better be naked here in kip
  "Than dressed in Lambeth Cut."

"One tanner more," the dressed man said,
  "One tanner says the word,
  "Off comes my coat of rat-catcher
  "And my breeches of velvet cord;

> "Now pull my shirt over my head,
> "I'm naked sole to crown,
> "And that's the end of fifty years
> Tobying up and down."
>
> A minute and they had changed about,
> And each had his desire;
> A dressed man and a naked man
> Stood by the kip-house fire.

*

The publication of *Burmese Days* in 1934 shows remarkable discipline. For a man for whom poetry had been an essential ingredient of his life since childhood, he indulges in only a two-line couplet to describe his main character's inadequacies.

> New-tick Flory does look rum,
> Got a face like a monkey's bum.

He had however, written various sonnets describing the pattern of his existence both before and after embarking on his first book, and which are mentioned elsewhere in this volume.

By 1934, Blair's life was undergoing great change; his literary ability was at last being recognized and his work published; he was living away from home allowing greater privacy in his private life; he was, despite unreliable health, feeling the strange pleasure of standing at a crossroads and surveying the various directions in which these new opportunities could take him. His reference to Buridan's ass (or donkey, as this poem describes it) refers to the donkey that died of starvation because it stood between two sources of food and could not decide which kind it preferred. The story is attributed to Jean Buridan, 14th century French scholar and philosopher,

'On a Ruined Farm Near the His Master's Voice
Gramophone Factory'
(*The Adelphi*, April 1934)

*

As I stand at the lichened gate
With warring worlds on either hand –
To left the black and budless trees,
The empty sties, the barns that stand

Like tumbling skeletons – and to the right
The factory-towers, white and clear
Like distant glittering cities seen
From a ship's rail – as I stand here,

I feel, and with a sharper pang,
My mortal sickness; how I give
My heart to weak and stuffless ghosts,
And with the living cannot live.

The acid smoke has soured the fields,
And browned the few and windworn flowers;
But there, where steel and concrete soar
In dizzy geometric towers –

There, where the tapering cranes sweep round,
And great wheels turn, and trains roar by
Like strong, low-headed brutes of steel –
There is my world, my home; yet why

So alien still? For I can neither
Dwell in that world, nor turn again
To scythe and spade, but only loiter
Among the trees the smoke has slain.

> Yet when the trees were young, men still
> Could choose their path – the wingèd soul,
> Not cursed with double doubts, could fly,
> Arrow-like to a foreseen goal;
>
> And they who planned those soaring towers,
> They too have set their spirit free;
> To them their glittering world can bring
> Faith, and accepted destiny;
>
> But none to me as I stand here
> Between two countries, both-ways torn,
> And moveless still, like Buridan's donkey
> Between the water and the corn.

*

This is the last poem that 'Eric Arthur Blair' wrote for *The Adelphi*. In December 1934 he began to call himself George Orwell to his friends, having changed his name for the publication of *Down and Out in Paris and London* in January 1933. He wrote reviews for *The Adelphi* throughout 1935 but did not lose himself in the rhythm of poetry again until the end of the year. By that time, when the contrasts between his growing stability and even celebrity, with that of the hardship and hunger of his self-imposed tramping days, began to cut deep into his conscience. The tone, the timbre, the pulse of Orwell's passions and beliefs seem to have taken a downward spiral during that year.

Orwell's third novel, *Keep the Aspidistra Flying*, was published by Victor Gollancz in 1936. The book hosts a poem that evolves slowly throughout 168 of its 277 pages, beginning with one shy little two-line couplet on page 5, and then growing verse by verse in every chapter, finally emerging in its entirety on pages 167-168. This is a unique and fascinating way to present a poem, involving the reader at every point of its evolution.

'St. Andrew's Day'
(*Keep the Aspidistra Flying*
Gollancz 1936)

*

'Sharply the menacing wind sweeps over
　　The bending poplars, newly bare,
　And the dark ribbons of the chimneys
　　Veer downward; flicked by whips of air;

　Torn posters flutter; coldly sound
The boom of trains and the rattle of hooves,
　And the clerks who hurry to the station
　　Look, shuddering, over the Eastern rooves;

Thinking, each one, "Here comes the winter!
　　Please God I keep my job this year!"
　And bleakly, as the cold strikes through
　　Their entrails like an icy spear;

　They think of rent, rates, season tickets,
　　Insurance, coal, the skivvy's wages,
Boots, school bills and the next instalment
　　Upon the two twin beds from Drage's;

　For if, in careless summer days
　　In groves of Ashtaroth we whored,
　Repentant now, when winds blow cold,
　　We kneel before our rightful lord;

　The lord of all, the money-god,
　Who rules us blood and hand and brain,
　Who gives the roof that stops the wind,
　　And, giving, takes away again;

> Who marks, with jealous, watchful care,
> Our thoughts, our dreams, our secret ways,
> Who picks our words and cuts our clothes,
> And maps the pattern of our days;
>
> Who chills our anger, curbs our hope,
> And buys our lives and pays with toys,
> Who claims as tribute broken faith,
> Accepted insults, muted joys;
>
> Who binds with chains the poet's wit,
> The navvy's strength, the soldier's pride,
> And lays the sleek, estranging shield
> Between the lover and his bride.'

*

Where did 'the groves of Ashtaroth' come from? Here is a distant echo from the past that Eric Blair had shared with Jacintha Buddicom, when Ashtaroth or Astarte, Goddess of Love, held them both in thrall. There was one more little four-line rhyme later on in the book, on page 257, guying the advertising world and describing itself thus. "There was a picture of a horribly eupeptic family, with grinning ham-pink faces, sitting at breakfast; underneath, in blatant lettering:

> Why should you be thin and white?
> And have that washed-out feeling?
> Just take hot Bovex every night –
> Invigorating – healing!"

*

A ray of sunshine appeared briefly when Orwell, in November 1936, wrote a review of 'Desert Encounter' by Knud Holmboe for *Time and Tide*, translated from the Danish by Helga Holbek. It feels as though he thoroughly enjoyed addressing this work which in turn inspired his own galloping verse, full of wit and sparkle, and suggests that life was being good to him at last, especially his sex life. Here is the upbeat Orwell, newly married on the 9 June 1936 to Eileen O'Shaughnessy, and now on the verge of offering up his life to justice and freedom in the Spanish Civil War. It appears to have been the only poetry he had time to write during this period as nothing more has come to light, apart from a few scribbled lines during the Blitz, until 1942.

'A Happy Vicar I Might Have Been'
(*The Adelphi*
December 1936)

*

A happy vicar I might have been
Two hundred years ago,
To preach upon eternal doom
And watch my walnuts grow;

But born, alas, in an evil time,
I missed that pleasant haven,
For the hair has grown on my upper lip
And the clergy are all clean-shaven.

And later still the times were good,
We were so easy to please,
We rocked our troubled thoughts to sleep
On the bosoms of the trees.

All ignorant we dared to own
The joys we now dissemble;
The greenfinch on the apple bow
Could make my enemies tremble.

But girls' bellies and apricots,
Roach in a shaded stream,

> Horses, ducks in flight at dawn,
> All these are a dream.
>
> It is forbidden to dream again;
> We maim our joys or hide them;
> Horses are made of chromium steel
> And little fat men shall ride them.
>
> I am the worm who never turned,
> The eunuch without a harem;
> Between the priest and the commissar
> I walk like Eugene Aram,
>
> And the commissar is telling my fortune
> While the radio plays,
> But the priest has promised an Austin Seven,
> For Duggie always pays.
>
> I dreamed I dwelt in marble halls,
> And woke to find it true;
> I wasn't born for an age like this;
> Was Smith? Was Jones? Were you?

In fact, throughout his life limericks and nonsense poetry had always appealed to Orwell, probably implanted in his mind by the limericks with which he and Jacintha had entertained each other in their teen years. Although there is no reference to these in *The Complete Works* because he did not share them with his family or school friends, there are a couple of examples to be found in *Eric & Us* by J. Buddicom, up-dated and republished with a postscript in 2006.[13] One of them is by Jacintha but the Cholmondeley/Chumly limerick, though not claimed as his work, is very much in Eric's style and deserves inclusion in these pages.

> A nervous young fellow named Cholmondeley
> Found his hard-boiled egg sandwich too crolmondeley.
> But his hostess, Miss Moore,
> Hated crumbs on the flore –
> So she didn't put up with him dolmondeley.

*

Remnants of this fractured verse, which he probably shared with his wife Eileen as they seem to have had a similar sense of humour, remained in his head because, during the Blitz in 1940, he would distract himself from the bombing and write in his diary little snippets that floated into his memory from childhood. [14]

> An old Rumanian peasant
> Who lived at Mornington Crescent

*

> And the key doesn't fit and the bell doesn't ring,
> But we all stand up for God save the King.

*

> When the Borough Surveyor has gone to roost
> On his rod, his pole or his perch ......

*

> Your mother was a spinster, say the bells of the Westminster,
> Don't keep talking balls, say the bells of St. Paul's.

*

The London Blitz gave Orwell plenty of time to contemplate, while sheltering with Eileen from the bombs which nightly rained down on the capital and its inhabitants. One such occasion resulted, after going back over his experiences in Spain, in the creation of a curiously intimate piece of verse.

'The Italian Soldier Shook my Hand' [15]
(Autumn 1942)

*

The Italian soldier shook my hand
　　Beside the guard-room table;
The strong hand and the subtle hand
　　Whose palms are only able

To meet within the sound of guns,
　　But Oh! what peace I knew then
In gazing on his battered face
　　Purer than any woman's!

For the flyblown words that make me spew
　　Still in his ears were holy,
And he was born knowing what I had learned
　　Out of books and slowly.

The treacherous guns had told their tale
　　And we both had bought it,
But my gold brick was made of gold –
　　Oh! who ever would have thought it?

Good luck go with you, Italian soldier!
　　But luck is not for the brave;
What would the world give back to you?
　　Always less than you gave.

Between the shadow and the ghost,
　　Between the white and the red,
Between the bullet and the lie,
　　Where would hide your head?

> For where is Manuel Gonzalez,
> And where is Pedro Aguilar,
> And where is Ramon Fenellosa?
> The earthworms know where they are.
>
> Your name and your deeds were forgotten
> Before your bones were dry,
> And the lie that slew you is buried
> Under a deeper lie;
>
> But the thing I saw in your face
> No power can disinherit:
> No bomb that ever burst
> Shatters the crystal spirit.

*

Orwell had, by this time, become literary editor of the journal *Tribune* and created a niche for his work entitled 'As I Please.' A great many of his collected essays were published under this title and when poet Alex Comfort, using a pseudonym, wrote a lengthy and provocative anti-war saga for *Tribune* entitled 'Letter to an American Visitor,' it presented a juicy carrot to entice Orwell into an equally lengthy, and furiously patriotic response, sub-titled 'A Letter to Obadiah Hornbooke.'

Because the following saga is so lengthy, I have taken the liberty of presenting just one of the fifteen stanzas of Alex Comfort's monumental epic so that you will understand a little better why Orwell flew into such a furious riposte, parodying the poet's layout and style. Alex Comfort was, in those days and always, a young pacifist and conscientious objector. He was still at University from which he eventually graduated in 1944 from Trinity College, Cambridge with a BA in Medicine, and then the Royal London Hospital with Conjoint diplomas; in all accruing six diplomas. He described himself as an aggressive anti-militarist and did not mince his words. From 'Letter to an American Visitor by Obadiah Hornbooke.' *Tribune* 4 June 1943 (Verse 12)

> Oh for another Duncaid – a POPE
> To purge this dump with his gigantic boot –
> Drive fools to water, aspirin or rope –
> Make idle lamp-posts bear their fitting fruit –
> Oh for another vast satiric comet
> To blast this wretched tinder, branch and root.
> The servile stuff that makes a true man vomit –
> Sucked from the works to which they cling like leeches,
> Those resurrection-puddings, Churchill's speeches.

The fifteen stanzas of Comfort's anti-war cant, with its aura of lofty distaste, must have been too much for Orwell. Disgusted by Comfort's disparaging tone, he responded with the full blast of a liberal vocabulary. And once he had started, there was no stopping him:

> 'As One Non-Combatant to Another.'
> (A Letter to Obadiah Hornbrooke)
> *Tribune*, 18 June 1943
>
> *
>
> O poet strutting from the sandbagged portal
> Of that small world where barkers ply their art,
> And each new "school" believes itself immortal,
> Just like the horse that draws the knacker's cart;
> Oh captain of a clique of self-advancers,
> Trained in the tactics of the pamphleteer,
> Where slogans serve for thoughts and sneers for answers –
> You've chosen well your moment to appear
> And hold your nose amid a world of horror
> Like Dr. Bowlder walking through Gomorrah.
>
> In the Left Book Club days you wisely lay low,
> But when "Stop Hitler" lost its old attraction

You bounded forward in a Woolworth's halo
To cash in on the anti-war reaction;
You waited till the Nazis ceased from frightening,
Then, picking a safe audience, shouted "Shame!"
Like a Prometheus you defied the lightning,
But didn't have the nerve to sign your name.
You're a true poet, but as saint and martyr
You're a mere fraud, like the Atlantic Charter.

Your hands are clean, and so were Pontius Pilate's,
But as for "bloody heads", that's just a metaphor;
The bloody heads are on Pacific islets
or Russian steppes or Libyan sands – it's better for
The health to be a CO than a fighter,
To chalk a pavement doesn't need much guts,
It pays to stay at home and be a writer
While other talents wilt in Nissen huts;
"We live like lions" – yes, just like a lion
Pensioned on scraps in a safe cage of iron.

For while you write the warships ring you round
And flights of bombers drown the nightingales,
And every bomb that drops is worth a pound
To you, or someone like you, for your sales
Are swollen with those of rivals dead or silent,
Whether in Tunis or the BBC,
And in the drowsy freedom of this island
You're free to shout that England isn't free;
They even chuck you cash, as bears get buns,
For crying "Peace" behind a screen of guns.

In 'seventeen to snub the nosing bitch
Who slipped you a white feather needed cheek,
But now when every writer finds his niche
Within some mutual admiration clique,
Who cares what epithets by Blimps are hurled?

Who'd give a damn if handed a white feather?
Each little mob of pansies is a world,
Cosy and warm in any kind of weather;
In such a world it's easy to "object,"
Since that's what both your friends and foes expect.

At times it's almost a dangerous deed
Not to object: I know, for I've been bitten.
I wrote in nineteen-forty that at need
I'd fight to keep the Nazis out of Britain;
And Christ! how shocked the pinks were! Two years later
I hadn't lived it down; one had the effrontery
To write three pages calling me a "traitor",
So black a crime it is to love one's country.
Yet where's the pink that would have thought it odd of me
To write a shelf of books in praise of sodomy?

Your game is easy and its rules are plain:
Pretend the war began in 'thirty-nine',
Don't mention China, Ethiopia, Spain,
Don't mention Poles except to say they're swine;
Cry havoc when we bomb a German city,
When Czechs get killed don't worry in the least,
Give India a perfunctory squirt of pity
But don't enquire what happens further East;
Don't mention Jews – in short, pretend the war is
Simply a racket "got up" by the Tories.

Throw in a word of "anti-Fascist" patter
From time to time, by way of re-insurance,
And then go on to prove it makes no matter
If Blimps or Nazis hold the world in durance;
And that we others who "support" the war
Are either crooks or sadists or flag-wavers
In love with drums and bugles, but still more
Concerned in catching Brendan Bracken's favours;

Or fools who think that bombs bring back the dead,
A thing not even Harris ever said.

If you'd your way we'd leave the Russians to it
And sell our steel to Hitler as before;
Meanwhile, you save your soul, and while you do it,
Take out a long-term mortgage on the war.
For after war there comes an ebb of passion,
The dead are sniggered at – and there you'll shine,
You'll be the very bull's-eye of the fashion,
You almost might get back to 'thirty-nine,
Back to the dear old game of scratch-my-neighbour
In sleek reviews financed by coolie labour.

But you don't hoot at Stalin – that's "not done" –
Only at Churchill; I've no wish to praise him,
I'd gladly shoot him when the war is won,
Or now, if there were someone to replace him.
But unlike some, I'll pay him what I owe him;
There was a time when empires crashed like houses
And many a pink who'd titter at your poem
Was glad enough to cling to Churchill's trousers
Christ! how they huddled up to one another
Like day-old chicks about their foster-mother!

I'm not a fan for "fighting on the beaches,"
And still less for the "breezy uplands" stuff,
I seldom listen-in to Churchill's speeches,
But I'd far sooner hear that kind of guff
Than your remark, a year or so ago,
That if the Nazis came you'd knuckle under
And peaceably "accept the *status quo*,"
Maybe you would! But I've a right to wonder
Which will sound better in the days to come,
"Blood, toil and sweat" or "Kiss the Nazis bum."

But your chief target is the radio hack,
The hired pep-talker – he's a safe objective,
Since he's unpopular and can't hit back.
It doesn't need the eye of a detective
To look down Portland Place and spot the whores,
But there are men (I grant, not the most heeded)
With twice your gifts and courage three times yours
Who do that dirty work because it's needed;
Not blindly but for reasons they can balance,
They wear their seats out and lay waste their talents.

All propaganda's lying, yours or mine;
It's lying even when its facts are true;
That goes for Goebbels or the "party line,"
Or for the Primrose League or PPU.
But there are truths that smaller lies can serve,
And dirtier lies that scruples can gild over;
To waste your brains on war may need more nerve
Than to dodge facts and live in mental clover;
It's mean enough when other men are dying,
But when you lie, it's much to know you're lying.

That's thirteen stanzas, and perhaps you're puzzled
To know why I've attacked you – well, here's why:
Because your enemies all are dead or muzzled,
You've never picked on one who might reply.
You've hogged the limelight and you've aired your virtue,
While chucking sops to every dangerous faction,
The Left will cheer you and the Right won't hurt you;
What did you risk? Not even a libel action.
If you would show what saintly stuff you're made of,
Why not attack the cliques you *are* afraid of?

Denounce Joe Stalin, jeer at the Red Army,
Insult the Pope – you'll get some come-back there;

> It's honourable, even if it's barmy,
> To stamp on corns all round and never care.
> But for the half-way saint and cautious hero,
> Whose head's unbloody even if "unbowed",
> My admiration's somewhere near to zero;
> So my last words would be: Come off that cloud,
> Unship those wings that hardly dared to flitter,
> And spout your halo for a pint of bitter.

*

If you've managed to survive those fifteen stanzas of ringing national pride, it is hard not to recognize that the stout young patriot aged eleven, who began this anthology with 'Awake Young Men of England' was still alive and kicking in the mature Orwellian breast. Contemptuous as he had been of Alex Comfort's stance as a conscientious objector, he still wrote Comfort a good-natured apology for such a public condemnation. This over-long diatribe proves incidentally to be quite informative concerning Orwell's own beliefs.

In 1944 Orwell published a poem recording his memories of the London Blitz (7 September 1940 – 21 May 1941). He was literary editor of *Tribune* for two years until 1945 and this poem appeared on 21 January.

'Memories of the Blitz'

*

> Not the pursuit of knowledge
> Only the chances of war,
> Led me to study the music
> Of the male and the female snore;
>
> That night in the public shelter
> With seats no pillow could soften,
> Where I fled, driven out of my bed
> By bombs too near and too often.

And oh! the drone of the planes
And the answering boom of the gun,
And the cups of tea in the dawn
When the flames outdid the sun!

That was so long ago,
Three years ago or nearly,
And more has perished than gas masks;
I could not tell you clearly

What there can be to regret
In a time of casual slaughter,
When the windows were empty of glass
And pavements running with water;

But the guns have changed their tune,
And the sandbags are three years older;
Snow has kissed the flesh
From the bones of the German soldier;

The blimp has a patch on its nose,
The railings have gone to the smelter;
Only the ghost and the cat
Sleep in the Anderson shelter,

For the song the sirens sang
Is sunk to a twice-told story,
And the house where the chartered accountant
Perished in headline glory

Is only a clump of willow-herb
Where I share my sorrow
With the deserted bath-tub
And the bigamous sparrow.

*

For those reading through this little volume who can recall those violent war years, *Memories of the Blitz* conjures up very sharply the sheer thunderous sound, the stench and blinding dust that those fifty-two nights of the 'Blitzkrieg' on London have left in those who took part in it. There are several poems within these covers which will surprise and stay in the memory, and this, for me at any rate, having been 'blitzed' and made homeless twice, is one of them.

With the publication of *Animal Farm* in 1945, Orwell's by now waning poetry output was briefly revived, firstly for Major, the old prize Middle White boar, to sing to the fractured melodies of 'Clementine' and 'La Cucuracha.'[16]

'Beasts of England'

Beasts of England, beasts of Ireland,
Beasts of every land and clime,
Hearken to my joyful tidings
Of the golden future time.

Soon or late the day is coming,
Tyrant Man shall be o'erthrown,
And the fruitful fields of England
Shall be trod by beasts alone.

Rings shall vanish from our noses,
And the harness from our back,
Bit and spur shall rust forever,
Cruel whips no more shall crack.

Riches more than mind can picture,
Wheat and barley, oats and hay,
Clover, beans and mangle-wurzels
Shall be ours upon that day.

> Bright will shine the fields of England,
> Purer shall its waters be,
> Sweeter yet shall blow its breezes
> On the day that sets us free.
>
> For that day we all must labour,
> Though we die before it break;
> Cows and horses, geese and turkeys,
> All must toil for freedom's sake.
>
> Beasts of England, beasts of Ireland,
> Beasts of every land and clime,
> Hearken well and spread my tidings
> Of the golden future time.

*

Eventually Old Major's anthem was replaced by a two-line couplet, composed by Minimus the poet pig, which was sung every Sunday.

> Animal Farm, Animal Farm,
> Never through me shalt thou come to harm.

Minimus the poet pig surpassed himself with a paean to the great Berkshire boar pig Napoleon, once the pecking order amongst the animals had been settled.[17]

> Comrade Napoleon

*

> Friend of the fatherless!
> Fountain of happiness!
> Lord of the Swill-bucket! Oh, how my soul is on
> Fire when I gaze at thy
> Calm and commanding eye,
> Like the sun in the sky,
> Comrade Napoleon.

> Thou art the giver of
> All that thy creatures love,
> Full belly twice a day, clean straw to roll upon;
> Every beast great or small
> Sleeps at peace in his stall,
> Thou watchest over all,
> Comrade Napoleon.
>
> Had I a sucking-pig,
> Ere he had grown as big
> Even as a pint bottle or as a rolling-pin,
> He should have learned to be
> Faithful and true to thee,
> Yes, his first squeak should be
> Comrade Napoleon.

*

There seems to have been a long gap in Orwell's poetic output after *Animal Farm* was published in 1945. So many major events took place in his life between 1944 and 1950, from the arrival of George and Eileen's adopted son Richard, aged three weeks, in June 1944 to Eileen's death in March 1945 while Orwell was away in Paris, busy being War Correspondent for *The Observer*. Despite the sporadic breakdowns in his health, he became very much in demand in this period and wrote copiously for *Tribune*, *The Observer*, etc and occasionally for periodicals such as *Partisan Review*, *Windmill*, and *Polemic*, to name but a few. The articles and essays were littered with quotations from the poetry of others, including that of poet T.S. Eliot, and it has been a problem picking out the very few lines of original verse from those of the work of other poets. After the tragically unexpected death of his wife Eileen, who died after an ovarian operation in March 1945, Orwell's work increased, apart from the time he spent with his baby son, Richard, from whom he refused to be parted. His health, always precarious, predictably deteriorated and the slide into full-blown tuberculosis began to take hold. Realising that the quality of the air in London was doing him no good, he embarked on a compromise of spending as much time as he could in the pure atmosphere of Scotland, at Barnhill, on the island of Jura. It was here that he was able to stretch and expand his imagination and create the nightmare scenario that was to become *Nineteen Eighty-Four*. There is a passage in this classic work that can surely be embraced as sheer poetry in prose, in the style of Orwell's most often quoted poet, T.S. Eliot. [18]

'Were there always these vistas of rotting nineteenth
century houses,
Their sides shored up with baulks of timber,
Their windows patched with cardboard and their roofs
with corrugated iron,
Their crazy garden walls sagging in all directions?
And the bombed sites where the plaster dust swirled
in the air
And the willow herb straggled over the heaps of rubble;
And the places where the bombs had cleared a larger patch
And there had sprung up sordid colonies of
wooded dwellings
Like chicken houses?
But it was no use. He could not remember.
Nothing remained of his childhood......' [19]

*

He appeared to be immersed in restless dissatisfaction, his moods swinging between sadness over the loss of Eileen; despair over his increasing ill-health; to delight in the fascinating development of his little son Richard and satisfaction with the constant call on his services, followed by frustration caused by the infrequency of physical relationships with various women friends. No original poetry attributed to Orwell can be found after the little poem in his essay 'Pleasure Spots', apart from repeats of poetry already published, until the last few days of his life.

On the 9th February 1949, Jacintha Buddicom, lifelong poet, mystic, humourist and by now forty-eight years old, wrote to Eric, on discovering that he had become George Orwell. There was an exchange of letters, and an invitation to visit him at Cranham Sanitorium, which made her hesitate so long that by the time she thought she just might accept the invitation, he had been moved to London and the moment was lost. Quite unexpectedly, that Autumn he announced his engagement to Sonia Brownell; they married on 13 October 1949 – and that was that. *Nineteen Eighty-Four* was published in June 1949, and within its pages have been found several four-line songs, taken from the far-off days of hop-picking in Kent, first related in detail in *Down and Out in Paris and London.* One of them in particular is worth recording as it gives a clue to the low state of his personal energy, the dwindling of his hope.

> Under the spreading chestnut tree
> I sold you and you sold me;
> There lie they, and here lie we
> Under the spreading chestnut tree.

*

At the very end, in the last days of his life, further indications of Orwell's failing spirit can be found in the scribbled rough draft of a poem which was never published until it was discovered by Peter Davison and included in *The Complete Works*, VOL XX. p210.

> Joseph Higgs, late of this parish,
> Who pushed the plough till he became the ploughshare,
> Exists no longer as the memory of a memory.
> His wooden graveboard vanished in a cold winter,
> A mishap with an inkpot blotted him from the register,

>   And – where the lost graves are visible,
>   Still
>   His raised right shoulder at the Day of Judgment
>   Might absolve him for the milkmaid's strangled daughter,
>   But
>   The middle years
>   When (boots were .... teeth were stumps of misery)
>   March mornings
>   Seven separate pains played in his body like an orchestra
>   Till
>   A dirty old man in a stinking cottage
>   Where the panes grew dark & the mice grew bolder.
>   Three days running no smoke from the chimneys
>   (burst the door in)
>   And broke his back to fit him in the coffin.
>   *Ne me perdas illa die*
>   (Either here or there – I would prefer it here, but let it be
>   there)
>   Without
>   I see no justification
>   For Joseph Higgs, late of this parish.

*

This sad scrawl, found in Orwell's last literary notebook, is a painful eye opener to the struggle he was having in clinging to his tragically short life during those last days of January 1950.

'Seven separate pains played in his body like an orchestra'

is surely the most agonizingly revealing sentence that ever came from this brilliant and, by now, exhausted mind. The whole fractured sequence of words are as if he is struggling for breath, searching in the dark for one more word – one more intake of air.

It was not to be. George Orwell died of a massive haemorrhage around 2.30 on the morning of 21 January 1950.

*

Abbreviations

CW   *The Complete Works of George Orwell*, edited by Peter Davison. Secker and Warburg. London 1998.
GO   George Orwell.
GO.EJL *George Orwell : Essays, Journalism & Letters.* Ian Angus and Sonia Orwell.

Textual Notes

1 – page iii – This poem does not appear, as might be imagined, in *Homage to Catalonia* but was written during the Blitz, in the Autumn of 1942 and published in *New Road* in June 1943.

2 – page 3 – GO: CW. Vol X.p 20-21. Cyril Connolly also wrote a 'Kitchener' poem and asked Eric to comment on it. The 'school's best poet' responded with – "*Dashed good. Slight repetition. Scansion excellent: Meaning a little ambiguous in places. Epithets for the most part well selected. The whole thing is neat, elegant and polished.*" Both boys were 13 at the time!

3 – page 7 – Bluebells and their pungent scent appeared several times in GO's work. The most explicit is to be found in *Nineteen Eighty-Four*, Part ll, chapter 1, page 124, when Winston has his first physical liaison with Julia.

4 – page 8 – See *Eric & Us: The Postscript Edition*, Finlay 2006. Postscript. page 180. para 2.

5 – page 9 – CW. Volume X, *A Kind of Compulsion* 1903-1936.

6 – page 10 – The Eton Wall Game is only played at Eton College, UK. It has a similarity to Rugby and a terminology of its own, not understood by most people! For details see Wikipedia online.

7 – page 15 – A 'wet bob' is an Eton pupil who plays sports involving water. A 'dry bob' is a pupil who plays other sports.

8 – page 19 – 1921. The Blair and Buddicom families

were enjoying the Summer holiday (mid July – early September) together renting a house called Glencroft in Rickmansworth, Hertfordshire. A few days before the end of the holiday, during a walk in the country lanes, Eric had attempted to make love to Jacintha in a rather more serious way than their usual embraces. Eric's unexpected passion had frightened Jacintha and, with torn clothing, she had run home and refused to speak to him again during last last few days of their holiday. It proved to be the end of their eight years together.

9 – page 22 – See GO: CW 1922-1927. 68. page 92.

10 – page 26 – See GO: CW Vol X. 1932. page 242. Note 123 re The Hawthornes private school.

11 – page 28 – Oliver Cromwell (1599-1658) military commander, self-named Lord Protector of England, Scotland and Ireland from 1653 until his death in 1658.

12 – page 31 – Booklovers' Corner, 1 Southend Road, Hampstead. London is now a pizza cafe.

13 – page 40 – See GO: CW. Vol XII 720. Wartime Diary – page 305.

14 – page 39 – *Eric & Us: The Postscript Edition.* Finlay. 2006 gives an up-to-date interpretation of the events described by Jacintha Buddicom in the 1974 edition of *Eric & Us*. It reveals and explains many of the points that Jacintha could not bring herself to share with her readers, including the reason for the friends' break-up.

15 – page 41 – See reference 1. page vi. 'The Italian Soldier Shook my Hand.'

16 – page 50 – 'Clementine' was an American folk song (Oh My Darling Clementine) possibly composed by H.S. Thompson. (1863)   'La Cucuracha' was a rousing ballad, sung to great effect by the very colourful Brazilian singer Carmen Miranda who was to be seen in many films during the 1940s-1950s, usually managing to sing and dance, balancing a cornucopia of fruit and stuffed birds on her head.

17 – page 51 –   See *Animal Farm.* Ch. Vlll. page 63.

18 – page 53 –   Style of T.S. Eliot's *The Waste Land.* From *Nineteen Eighty-Four;* page 5 – para 2.

19 – page 53 –   The remains of this quotation finishes "…. except a series of bright-lit tableaux, occurring against no background and mostly unintelligible." See *Nineteen Eighty-Four*, Part 1, page 5, para 2, lines 10-19.

20 – page 53 –   published in *Tribune*, 11 January 1946 in the section 'As I Please', a discussion on Nature and Man's Pleasures. Vol 4. *Orwell Essays, Journalism & Letters.* Orwell & Angus.

INDEX OF FIRST LINES

A dressed man and a naked man, 31
A happy vicar I might have been, 38
And the key doesn't fit, and the bell doesn't ring, 40
A nervous young fellow named Cholmondeley, 40
Animal Farm, Animal Farm, 51
An old Rumanian peasant, 40
As I stand at the lichened gate 34

Beasts of England, beasts of Ireland, 50
Brush your teeth up and down, brother, 23
By light, 19

Come up, Come up, ye kindly waves, 4

Dear Friend: allow me for a little while, 19

Empty as death and slow as pain, 23

Friend of the fatherless, 51
Friendship and love are closely intertwined, 18

Good people all, this is a joyous time, 28

Here lie the bones of poor John Flory; 27
Hills we have climbed and bogs we have sat in, 13

I am a wet bob who was trying to play cricket, 15
If you can keep your face, when all about you 10

Joseph Higgins, late of this parish, 54

My love and I walked in the dark, 25

New-tick Flory does look rum, 33
No stone is set to mark his nation's loss, 2
Not a breath is heard, not a moving of lip, 14
Not the pursuit of knowledge, 48

Oh! Give me the strength of the lion, 1
Oh, what can ail thee, loafer lorn, 12
O poet strutting from the sandbagged portal, 43
Our Minds are married, but we are too young, 9

Sharply the menacing wind sweeps over, 36
So here are you, and here am I, 7
Sometimes in the middle autumn days, 28
Summer-like for an instant the autumn sun bursts out, 30

The Italian soldier shook my hand 41
The Mariner blesseth the wind; the sun shone out,
    the clouds went down, 16
Three beggars begged by noon & night, 5

Under the spreading chestnut tree, 54

When I was young and had no sense, 20
When the Borough Surveyor has gone to roost, 40
When the Franks have lost their sway, 20
Were there always these vistas of rotting nineteenth
    century houses, 53
Why should you be thin and white? 37
Who is the mighty Captain? Who is he, 9

You mother talks balls, say the bells of St. Paul's, 40

Acknowledgements

Considering the modest size of this little volume, I have a great many people to thank for their help and support in bringing these pages to the reader. Because *George Orwell: The Complete Poetry* had to be presented as simply and sympathetically as possible, a whole phalanx of proof readers cast their eyes and red pencils over it. Thank you so much: Guy Loftus, Jane Monroe, and Ahdil Ravi. An extra special vote of thanks go to Lizzie Dymock and Julian Hodgson for considerable extra advice and unfailing support in the face of initial uncertainty, when occasionally their encouragement was a greater shot in the arm than reaching for a restorative glass of the amber liquid. Thanks and warm gratitude goes to Gordon Bowker for contributing the blurb on the cover and writing a review for The Orwell Society's *Journal*.

Finally, and with my deepest gratitude of all, warm thanks go to Peter Davison, not only for agreeing to write a preface to the anthology, but also for his firm but gentle words of wisdom and never-failing encouragement in this attempt to bring another level of understanding of George Orwell to those who read and respect his genius.

D.V.